CAREEN

grace shuyi liew

CAREEN

grace shuyi liew

Cover Photo: Human Chuo tying Gluwur, photo by Oscar
Book Cover & Interior Design: Sarah Gzemski

Published by Noemi Press, Inc. A Nonprofit Literary Organization.
www.noemipress.org.

INDEX

WHAT DOES IT MEAN TO BE DURATIONAL, NOT ETERNAL? // 9

EVENTUALLY EVERY COLOR CAREENS INTO ITS OWN LACK // 13

UNTITLED // 23

OUTGROWTH OF CONTINGENT NATIONS // 25

       ARS POETICA // 27

       PART I: // 28

       PART II: // 39

IF THIS IS NOT POSSIBLE, LIVE TWICE // 51

DISPLACED, REPLACED // 53

       BERLIN // 55

       NEW YORK // 57

       (BETWEEN) LOS ANGELES & OTHER COASTS // 59

       KUALA LUMPUR // 60

IN EVENT OF A PLUNGE, GIVE OVER TO YOUR BODY // 63

GOOD NIGHT, FALL IN— // 67

ALLUSIONS AGAINST TIME // 70

POSTLUDE // 73

THE USE OF LYRICISM //

NOTES // 85

ACKNOWLEDGEMENTS // 87

WHAT DOES IT MEAN TO BE DURATIONAL, NOT ETERNAL?

In this state, my opacity blooms
like wrong
soap
frothing out of a
dishwasher. White foam coats
my dreams
of fascism, alien abductions, and anywhere
but home

> The video games I prescribe myself click
> and lock me
> into place:
>
> I'm on a quest for a specific wild berry bush
> I'm getting attacked by mutated wolves
> I'm entering tunnels littered with gems
> I'm looting corpses
>
> I'm hearing voices.

I have since moved from a house by the train tracks to
another house
by another train tracks and every
night the train horn wakes me at
    6am;
    5am;
    3am;
tricks me
into believing the earth
is shattering from its
core
& I wish only
for this resounding
ache to carry
on in silence
instead

> I wish the train
> would blow up or
> roll off its rails

I can't be loud
when Asian porn is still
a consumer category,
milk-white skin like
a reverse oil spill
I survey the situation.
Accident, or pillaging?
Asian women
headlining all these
forward-thinking
genres, artificially
intelligent but lonely
& fixated
at simulation.
Our assigned
database of
gloom always comes
true. Our worries
nothing
but sincere. All our
automatic and negative
thoughts pass
the Turing test,
our joie
de vivre is
embedded
into code—a
lifelong hunt for
one family of origin:
itchy crotches,
curdled balls,
sexual services on
a fevered train,
back of an oxcart,
rickshaw to the middle
of nowhere, slipping
from age to age
in perpetuity
always hovering
at the outskirts
of a grand
unifying theory

There's an old desk in my bedroom I like to hide under
when I drift too far from my familiar horrors.
Find me there as a child,
dough-like and ready to rise
into shape for anyone who arrives with a threat
to take my life
if I don't go dead like a scare
crow. Upright and flaring
after the last crow
has fled my owner enters and coos:
Where is my little rainbow hiding this time?
Her taunts scrape
the undersides of my ache. I talk
wild shit to get dragged out
am made to squat in wait then forbidden
to touch myself. Still I do because I want
a beating, want to welt
backward into small openings all over
my skin asking
to be filled. I am asking for it when
my personal God wields a belt
like mama did. At what age do we
talk to our children about when
to fuck, why to take chances, and how to
outlive love? Who encoded the planned
obsolescence of an emotion?
I want her to never
stop. I am nine and high
out of my mind, wigged out on begging
for more or maybe I am seven and
about to be killed, or I am already
buried at twenty-
eight and cannot discern
the outlines of my cadaver oozing into earth,
nothing
if not a raw nerve ready
to graft onto anyone who comes
for me in a fury. Where my body ends and where
mama's begins
lies the rape that had
no space to exist. When I grow up I want
a fantasy. I reenact rape fairytales
with white lovers, all of whom

insist on hating Trump
while they fuck me—their rage
about The Administration dignifies
into a hard-on slinging
for my civic rights. Why so angry?
I ask. Blowjobs don't cost much
more than falling
in love with anyone
who expresses outrage on my behalf—
always when I lift my shirt to reveal
my private galaxy of
bruises
they all cum immediately

  (This glow is not unnatural.
   It's a dispersal happening at some
   indeterminable decay rate—have you ever
   seen the sun at dusk crowning a lighthouse?
   Call it a trace glimmer but it will set too and
   that's when all platitudes go dark)

                I learned of a courageous girl ready to jump off a cliff

                  Sitting on a rock ledge, she chatted for hours
                  with those pulling for her when someone said,
                  think of your mother. That edict gave her the
                  sincerity to finally push herself into thin air

We learn bodily ire from our mothers—how to run
out of our own flesh—

EVENTUALLY EVERY COLOR CAREENS INTO ITS OWN LACK

This original absence

In a hard-hearted era flood lights have replaced human observation.
See white widen. See difficulty describing architecture by geometry.
When revolving doors halt their spinning, it's the shifting lines that vex,
until every movement approaches music & no one remembers stopping.

Anger is never private. It resides directly above every common pulse
so that those who keep their eyes trained on clouds slowly lose their rage.
Even in old age our darkened hair only approximates lightness,
never fully lifting against the iron pull of bright fade.

If we refuse white space as instituted home, only to hear repudiations
fall like darkness, if we refuse to recognize our derived selves
& prefer instead the kind of beauty that will never absolve
meaning, if we keep gunning for what cannot bring change—

Will the pull of rage be gentle the way we tread above other people's heads
in an upstairs apartment? This is how lonesomeness paces its strides,
equipped by quiet. Even if we slip back down to earth our tiptoes will
never regain the dexterity for sliding heavy things in the dead night again.

To the first man who penetrated the sound barrier:

                                    how did

it feel
up there? Was the full, pressing
quiet
a melody
from a different life, before sounds
acquired color,
before silence signified
lack?

Did you feel a
strength to
invert
everything you knew about

                  space?
                  Did you bring back
                  some textures? Maybe
                  one day I can touch them too.

In another city I wake every morning at four

       My body drops to the floor to a time
       as a child, when I napped
       in the pillow of my sister's flesh, our hot backs losing

heat to the concrete
floor

of cold-
hardened veins, one of many
ways to expand

Sometimes, a neighbor's window lights up.
       I was not the only one keeping track of my
       crawling, when you told me about the years,

Years you have watched me, a hooded
       figure passing through dark doors, talking
       to her dry dinners, cursing the house plant,

falling to
drape over my yellowed chair the way chickens drop their

                     flattened necks onto plates

The house plant has no name.

The house plant generates its own light.

The house plant gets its water and nutrients from the air.

When I try to adapt to the environment by twisting
       toward abandonment it's

easier instead to imagine a man watching me from nowhere

Might nowhere regenerate? Mornings scattered into a few directions—

Someone's in our house.

    But you seem so big! Please—fold back into yourself—

My shadow, as a girl, lengthening alongside. Today is
   a permutation that relies as much on seclusion as technique:
how to curl, how to wane, how to make mazes out of a
    hunger that runs through stacked lives, mothers filtered

& reincarnated into strangers
             who only want to buy you.

Then, if the wind lifts your skirt, your conscience is strewn.
Into the frigid air your skin
dims,

purity passing from hand to white hand as currency.

    Didn't she say so?

No?

To have survived a life of gentle skirt-lifting is to never reap the joy of underexposure.

To retain a place in this world, burnish cherries until its red turns glossy with spit.

To people who gender the unborn what about the lotus is tagged with serrated lines.

To engineer a clear sky some nations swallow clouds and spike their rain.

To be tongued a floor has to retain its modesty even under duress.

To unfurl into a spread always keep the kneecaps ready at a moment's notice.

To collect hate colonialize first a chorus of white-bellied weeping.

To colonialize is to replenish the gaping cavity that once held the guts of a whole generation.

To force open the tenderness of a girl's fate push her underwater and wait; eventually the air bubbles will stop rising.

I was taught to content in intense instruction:

To ask life if its goal is to astonish or commit decay into rote.

I was taught bowing all the way toward those walks in evenings:

I never knew how benign standing upright was, until I did it one day.

I was taught the relief of being wrong:

When translation fails, the displaced easily become worthless beings.

But this idea of the barren abruptly baring all

of itself when alarmed by intimacy

does not tidy up easy. I was left to tug at myself for too long

Remaining inert saved my life

UNTITLED

after Anne Sexton

As for me, I am a watercolor.
I wash off.
Some nights I dream
I am monument & eternal
& you, human,
at the base of my stairs.
I cannot deny
you permission because
I am standing too
tall, too wanting
to be helpless
against your peeling
stare, my shell
an open entrance for
the validated ticket
stub in your hand
& no,
it is not a violation, not
in any legal or
philosophical sense
at least, not against any
planetary order,
& if morality
is a mortal
construct no more
everlasting
than the
monolithic statues &
shrines & soft hearts of human
society, then I am water
color lifting
into ether. I am hard
to stain.
I wash off.

OUTGROWTH OF CONTINGENT NATIONS

A tale of statelessness

ARS POETICA

after Rosmarie Waldrop

In your narrow room
living from a suitcase
packed silent adjustments
every permission
you give & custom
make to order when
you were born
once faraway
saying "tree" when
you meant "three"
then born again easy
to correct as strength
answering any dim
question for new
appearances arguing
away ideals once visible
communicate is hazy
revelation in stone green
specific dead body
dislodging yourself a prized
collection display
whatever's hurled at you
behind you
find the quality of
a thing in the world
never existed a time
unencumbered
by subjectivity
who does "you"
stand for henceforth?

PART I:

The body's melancholia falls in love by flaunting its talent for mimicking grace (or sheerness) (arduous passes) (lit/vanished lit/vanished) No one taught you (yet you know) how to preserve a love (your palms leaking slices of light) how your role is always to await spoilage (hushed under airtight thighs / yanked from a hiding place / pacified to the tune of a white pulse) Let me see, let's see: how mimicry nurses melancholy / how every skip of your dropped heart attunes to stillness (shhh).

To ask for likeness in exchange for lightheartedness is an unnecessary cruelty. You've been there before: paper planes that won't fold themselves (unthinkable to defy a birthright / impossible to rise out of flatness), a face that parades singularity. You would really love to keep on living. You would really love to forget the past (straighten out those bends in your yester-limbs). The people you have _____ or _____ or _____ line up to ring your doorbell with questions; their decoys walk right through the walls of your home.

One came into this world holding sour
                    in her nose,   an event / animal

        on whose tail rode every time-abiding claim

To peel off insistence she rolled in
grass, citronella and blue star, though
under a sky that's always curving
                    she would never again return to scent

For the day
        beneath a thousand lamps lit in accident

she waited
        to ride out of a bright night forest / abandon
        all incoming movements / hear unborn
        bodies clap at their reflections

        Sensing wind

        Sensing wind

        Sensing a swallowing wind

As arid as my mouth

            Sucking on your name

Here are specks of hunger surfacing from a white floor, here is the most organic portal into a margin.

***

The portal opens only from the inside, a useable meat hole, a time before the ancient west spat out mythologies that named the planets, forever spoiling their constitutions.

***

What's left behind since then trembles faintly at the edges—an idea without an outline.

***

Too many have heard of the woman on the moon.

Too few remembered.

Women in our legends are always flying off.

How damp are the nights up there?

How celestially ordained your flight?

They will teach you to distrust, as if children cannot—will not—do harm.

***

Who regards you as liberation?

Why do they offer to wipe your face?

***

Those who carry within them a recessed space all know their place.

Line each dent up to find that no two look the same.

Oily, gritty, underfoot. Unfixed thinghood.

You expect consensual captivity of your body to bring you refuge the way every sick rendition of (universal) truth needs a savage figure (original parts of a whole) in order to imagine freedom. Sex between ciswomen is mirrored geography (or out-of-date adage) (?) Bending at the waist (either backward or forward) is still an imprecision so ingrained it can only evoke bondage (take it) or charity (asking for it). Neither satisfies a Syaitan spinning yarn. When permission (giving away power) weaves into objectification (receding humanity) the fist in your heart drops its punch (forgo return to another country).

Mark your presence out in the wild.

You are face up, physically open,

       perilous next to cracks in the weather,
       familiar expressions emerging out of a rockface
       cut by moonlight.

The edges will always be dimmed.

In this natural phenomenon: Specter of a small girl, half-beaming, splashing in a green lake, her dark hair cropped at mid-cheek, her memory of her mother scant.

       Inside you is a mother wounded from the death of her mother.

       Inside her is a mother who never recovered from the birth of
       her children.

See how water parts for her.

Before we fell into our form there were other stories that waited
around.

The descriptions return now and again the way a finch searches the
snow
in a deceptively simple landscape of total whiteness,

desperation guised as a linger:

      always about to flit, never to flit.

***

Hair, first hair, dipped in black of irises.

All of us unmoored by the charge of
benevolence.

You are gonna be okay you say (closed in by bodies) (imaginary pangs) as you familiarize yourself with the facts of your dislocation. You were never clean: your denouncements have always been (mis-)taken as unhinged (orbits of a soft mind). Not that you didn't earnestly imagine pleasure at every chance (fumbling at your own body) (an avatar made swollen by a grimy appetite) (pliant tongues lapping through a chest opening). You lie spreadeagle and through your teeth to pacify (/investigate) movements that reverberate. (Awaiting the day all your fingers end up inside yourself.)

PART II:

I have heard of extinction; I just don't aspire to ruin. When lichen started blooming under my nails I hired a lawyer who referred me to a federal officer to discuss signs of spiritual withdrawal. When asked *are you of sound mind* I rounded my mouth into an O like I'm the heroine of a silent film; God was moved to sit with me by the sidewalk, pro bono. He nullified my deposition effectively immediately. I saw ridges spiking out of clouds that day; balance or be toppled is the cumulated message from the higher-ups. Meanwhile moss has seeped into my cuticles; time carries on. In the nonchalant building, past the metal detector, at the back of a long line of second language speakers, I encounter a confused child. His speech is nationless as he wobbles toward anyone who also held something in their hands; my toy soldier for your cell phone, sir? Why wouldn't anyone trade their hand-thing with his hand-thing? Why do some hand-things carry more intrinsic worth than others? At midnight all the telephone lines go dead. My name called wrongly is still my name, until each incorrect letter bears out its worthless existence indefinitely.

Others will always want to know if you speak languages you don't speak; hitch you to a framework; aerate you into helplessness.

Make a ghost of your poise.

A circle of desire digging from inside another bigger circle is predetermined to forage ceaselessly until it encounters a warm opening, only to mistake it for recognition.

I take walks alone now.

Without a palm to advise bruises, I am lashed instead by solitude under a late afternoon sky.

Mirroring others to find myself only leads to invisibility.

The proof of my suffering dissolves at the end of each day, no matter how sturdy the day's buildup.

An entire subcontinent kneeled before the execution, before the sky turned before our eyes, before the whole lot of us vanished.

Placidity idled like an upright hoe meanwhile.

Carefree is one form of amnesia.
A shit requirement. Even soft
wind contains a larger assembly
that make up its buoyant
face-kissing quality
When I think about being
freed of care the way sludge
slopping the bottom of your
coffee cup never worries
about its revolting state
the exertive parts of my
previous lives are backed
into the vanished corners
they came from—
back through chipped-
off tombstones &
hopeless spindles
made from deadwood
Anywhere I go my face
becomes a gathering
space for other people's
regressed ideas of carefree
If Lady Justice did
once upon a time wear pigtails
and lift her skirt for the winds
before she settled into
statuehood maybe
it's true there is no such thing
as an uncontainable wound,
only events that have asked
to go off the historical record

I drove my car into the sea-green sky
Highway flanked by lucid freshwater
I had so many times solemnly
sworn to Saint of Sad Archives
to tell the whole truth
My right palm raised
like a citizen
My left fist wound tight
around a purchased promise
Behind the bureaucrat's door yet
      another banal man wipes his face blank
      while he approves some good news
      from the Homeland Security
      mechanically I loved him too
      with the open lust
      trapped whales feel for humans
      who dive into the ocean biting knives
      to cut their fishing nets loose
Envelopes carrying all my imminent
paperwork were shipped
to the middle of this country
where the average processing wait time
cannot be guaranteed to exist
Terrifyingly normal men who
carry out their methodical task to preserve
the united states in its midnight hour
Breathless, timeless
Just waiting for the smallest item
on a long checklist to go wrong
I have tried to collect
all the bad
jokes clotting the air
Whole
skies of feathers
bagged one by one
into documentation
I gritted my teeth until
they fell loose each enamel
to be labeled as one more
piece of evidence
thrown into the container
strapped to my back

The manmade lake tills life into the white bellies of its fish.

The ability to situate oneself flashes in between muted images—a quick shimmer, a stifled rustle, some blood staining a pinhole on the back of a hand.

By the lake I read about the colonial farming of the color blue. How fallen skies were mapped onto a white girl's petticoat. How slaves gave birth to a sky's hue.

An unseen sigh breaks open the water's surface.

To soothe my sense of loss, I force myself down a hallway designed to be invisible to people like me.

Part of the narrative requires incomprehension.

When smelling a field of jagged afternoon light, the heart shrinks and surges upward to demand likeness—from a sky just beginning to crack.

I try to recall something I cannot possibly have a firsthand memory of.

It's not that I think abstractions cannot fulfill justice; it's just;

The things passed down pelt us like hail on a sulky summer night; like discrete units of grief; like an inventory of conquests; like entire alternated lives;

It is grain by grain by grain that we offer comfort.

So: Apply spit to gloss the tarnished. Return to our maker this fear of falling.

That season, you declared your inclination to eat
everything within reach, snap-closing a coin purse emptied
of usefulness. This flatscape, coniferous. The first winter
of slack winds. The badlands tracking you back through
doors you'd long ago torn off. Their hinges were still sucking on the
entryways, each bare surroundings whiter than dirt. Slowly your
steel face
began to trickle, unbroken the way of water, until the long day
aimed its arrow south of you. You could have worried more given
the facts of your life, but your heart distended
in order to learn fear. An uplift is bitterness homebound.

For the fact that you will never again encounter an entire continent of people hushed to a fault. For the fact that the pulse low on your spine is already hardening despite its need. For the fact that night heat rises inside you like an airlift. For the fact that you are already someone else looking back in time. For the fact that you rounded down into a bowl to carry your mother's worry. For the fact that you will never outgrow alienation. When you learn to question if anguish must stick around as supplication, if bodies must accumulate peril over time, if the end of your name is really knotted to a red string carrying the stories from your many lifetimes—you will find that when power cultivates its own logic, you will never choose the right path when the road ahead forks. Poetry isn't located in aftermaths, and the ties that bind are all banal; only you can find mercy in a bitterness swelling to choke all exit doors.

In this formation the snow is
jagged, even though by nature

cold water breaks shapes. Just how
natural laws turn aberrant sometimes,

gale-mother chancing lone, paled by
commotion and its din of signified

worth. I want to ruin your life
it's said. So the frost in its black

wet might want to numb
a revolution. Else why else

come up from under the covers,
as if love would move beyond

displeasing for just anyone? ---- No.
Abide. Even the gloom

in a puddle has origins in ease, so
then I will still eat from your palm

in the dark. I will still aberrate
like a good girl just beneath

your hoodwinking breasts.
Somehow mothering in this climate

feels opulent. Or it's just
spilled ice marking myself up

as dislocated, two/three spheres of
bodies spat out of a lack of friction,

such readinesses so
interminable I hunger

to gather for return
all the names you have given me.

What if sometimes, I just want an awakening?
The kind the size of a parking lot, no bigger.

Who in your life has endured harms you wish you could undo?

Lighted cries increasing density

If I had known that ledges take their time to widen and flatten

Get off me get off me get off me get off me

I struggle to find a sustainable container for my words

My cheap gaze to keep you less lonely

The strive against stratified basin—
So many things about the natural world I have yet to learn

IF THIS IS NOT POSSIBLE, LIVE TWICE

after Mary Ruefle's "Some Nondescript Autumn Weekend"

A poet's advice:

    Step one: Remove everything beautiful from your home
    Step two: Leave behind everything ugly, disgusting, painful, repulsive, grotesque, hated
    Step three: Live inside this ghastly space
    Step five: At the end of sixty days, empty the space, wash it clean
    Step six: Live inside this cleaned blank space
    Step seven: At the end of sixty days, bring back only the beautiful things
    Step eight:

My questions for the poet:

    To what do you consent once you are surrounded
    by superlatives of your own arranging?

    To whom do you give the potential to seize the whole space of you?

    From whom do you ask for changes in scenery?

DISPLACED, REPLACED

Cityscapes of halfways

BERLIN

Arrangement is luck. You wake up one morning to a swollen top lip. Each day you stare in the mirror at a face formed and reformed by disparity. Probably a combination of bad sleep, lack of fruit in your diet, and inertia. Or an infection of a two-month-old lip piercing, right in the cupid's bow of your mouth.

Berliners apologize to you, a voyeur, for the gray December skies. You are three days away from the longest night of the year. By 4pm it's pitch dark. The right conditions can split wide open what's self-evident. Your top lip, puffy as a newborn's cheek, marks you. You are free to appear safe to others. Embedded under that lip is an assurance of evaporation.

The white pus is wet and persistent.

Google tells you to check for heat at the affected location. Gargle saltwater to purge possible infection. You order milchkaffees at cafes and flirt with women and forget to check for pain or redness or possible cures. When you remember you push your index finger against your lip and white pus crawls out like a fat worm. You can't talk much or move your lips, becoming newly private as the proprietor of diminishing smiles.

An ex emails you about under-bridge parties with marginalia reminders of the ways this city gestures at despair that amount to universal hospitality. If you are a girl dispersing into invisible mental fragments, then you didn't attend the bridge party, didn't kiss a perfect-skinned German girl and fall into her translucence.

In spite of your disappearing face, in spite of your swollen top lip, you let your white-loving splinter bury itself further under your skin.

You angle for perfect eyebrows. White women wish you a happy morning that day you slept only three hours. On the U-Bahn your eyes well up. Observation originated from cities, and you only want to listen. To see is to approximate the source of lack, and teary eyes become fully functional, may even recreate perception.

In another way you have been displaced before the time of the city.

You used to travel well. Now you wear your body as infiltration. The exchange of spaces occupies you up to the last unvetted thought. People unwilling to remain in sadness wear their bodies as readily charged, ready to flex violence against the other bodies entering their spheres.

You cross when it's red and yell in Chinese at a car screeching to a halt. You know how language flattens lives, but not knowing German gives you a dimensional armor.

You make yourself enter every one of them even though the English bookstores haunt you. The roof of the building is misshapen under the white weight of expatriates hungry for the Beats, the Lost Generation, the Brat Pack. Exile does not discriminate privacy. You add some color and gender variance to the window displays. The feminine mystique takes pride in chewing with sealed lips.

A British-accented owner asks about your lip, directs a customer toward Bret Easton Ellis.

You sneak a book of poetry under your parka into the hail and rain.

A market crowds the Berlin wall. *What do you see when you see me*, you want to grab a person by the elbow and back them into a wall.

Anger can froth some mobility into sadness, even if not all sadness is static. With some lag you group all your fears into a tall white wall you forget about and repeatedly knock into. The spiders in a recurring dream scuttle toward the wall, then scale it with ease.

A *New Yorker* critic of Berlin's Memorial to the Murdered Jews of Europe invites his reader to envision this: Germany affecting sincerity through individual citizens, each carving one of six million names onto the cement blocks. When you visit at night the children are still skipping in penitence. Why should it have been left unmarked? Why prize the pristine gray of a blank slate over candor? Who reads the *New Yorker*?

There is a naiveté in isolation. What does it mean to share a birth country? *Your fingers curl outward instead of inward.* This is how your mother valorizes with guilt your unflinching strut away from your family.

You have no desire to infantilize the trope of the mother. Here are your movements flinted with forgottenness, disallowed any intervention. You become attached to the swell in your lip. On the last day you did fix your gaze on a stranger: *Tell me about the last time you were unhappy with me.*

NEW YORK

The bus pulls into Chinatown before anyone has risen for the day. Rows of shop shutters rattle behind the freezing white mist. The cold slaps you into place.

In less than a day the year will turn over and burn.

Duality applies here: most alone, most accompanied. Most enclosed, most vast. Most filthy, most pure.

Closest to death, closest to not yet dying.

Your small, bright orange suitcase barely fits under the metal turnstile. Your train rattles toward your next destination.

You come up on the sidewalk dotted with black stains—skeptical but not idle, not contradicted against what is sought. Nothing but to begin doubting.

Emerging is one of your favorite things to do. You could walk up and out of an underground station forever.

In this language the words to signify the people dear to you are too singular. You are here to see old friends. You are here to remember. By the time you have lined up the correct metaphors to approximate the layers of how you feel, the feeling has already changed into a different feeling.

Again you slip back into refusing to recognize faces.

At the New Year's Eve party you are too busy mapping the contours of time to stall with small talk. To assimilate is to have regressed past the point of inhumanity.

By the moment of drunken hunger, past midnight, kissed twice, you are incoherent and sobbing: I am not one of you. I cannot say why. I speak all the ways you ask of me, but this one I cannot say why.

To frame noise as extraneous to knowledge is to be stuck in the process of awakening. Perpetually regaining self-consciousness. The slightest siren, thinnest rubbish truck beep, faintest titter around street corners, barely discernible.

But why should it have been you to cry?

57

What triggers the contagion of decay is not its desire to fall away but its insistence on renouncing rapture. Now, no one can delight. No one sings. Even the scraps of paper rubbish scissoring air are silent. Days later we fall out of bed together. Nothing changes in the morning.

On the last day of your visit you take a train to the airport but arrive in a taxicab. Your eyes, thickened from the journey, knock over the bartender's. She sends you a stiff drink, for free, then keeps her back to you until you drain your glass and climb off the barstool.

All the planes are on time.

(BETWEEN) LOS ANGELES & OTHER COASTS

You are falling, falling, easy as the way alleyways here seem to curl into one another.

At any moment, something drops into view. You try your best to read the messages within each appearing-disappearing vision. It was Frida Kahlo who declared, *I never painted dreams. I painted my own reality.* She wanted more than the fog of an easy legacy. If only she could wrestle herself back into her autobiography, strain clear the muddled myth-ification of perfectly ordinary insanity.

Even in sleep, you hear the crashing waves, loud and polite all night long.

The dream isn't larger than life. There is no such thing as empty dream.

On the French coastline you dream about the word 'riviera.' Bring a scene from some forgotten movie: noir shadows, aching red nails, and a puffy fog of lies lit by a single midnight street lamp. You can live for this loneliness, you think. Something will move if you just stared hard enough at a flat image.

You think 'ocean' means the possibility of becoming anything in the distant future. Any moment now, that roar and din at the back of your head will grow louder. You're counting on it to knock you over.

At the corner shop you ask *do you sell condoms* and the French shop girl brings a soup ladle. You try to say *ha-ha that will work too*, but no one understands your joke. You try another way and exaggerate surprise. The universal language of emptying your face: *I know nothing.* The shop people sense the hovering levity and giggle tentatively, then roar into laughter after you pull up Google Translate.

It's only because sex is funny, not you.

And where does that leave you and your overcompensating intonation?

After all the ready lies you have told, it's hard to keep track of what you actually want, where you hope to go. You get used to this hardness until your voice scabs over.

Mentally, you experience the subtropical coast as fragments—each element breaks down according to some atomic order. You aren't supposed to *see* the vibrations, but under a certain setting light of sun, everything trembles, and you—you believe everything you see, you are easy like that.

KUALA LUMPUR

The home state nurses a thirst for revenge that rages through your twenties. You return each year to steep like a teabag in muddy waters, eventually oversaturating the original means of holding. *Gimme just one reason why*, Tracy Chapman taunts, as the childhood heat swaths you like a christening gown. Even strapped down you remain manic for retaliation.

Look out the window. Hear the ambiance of small commands. People making and taking orders, calling one another brother, boss, babe, each sound taking you closer to a nexus planted on the side of your heart. No one is asking you to remember but you still feel excavated. You left, you went, you wanted to change a life, whose? Thinking of *heritage* makes you think of guitar riffs, the way they askto stay and be forgotten as soon as the next refrain.

As much as you want to remember, the past is mostly constructed by sounds, adik, and rarely does overcoming has to do with visual memory. There's that other truism—how it's only upon looking back that we realize we stayed somewhere longer than we should have—except we always forget how we hoarded nostalgia and made it hard to leave to begin with. That is another problem altogether, separate from language.

Right before the plane lands, you are greeted by never-ending acres of palm trees, tender fronds paralyzed in the humidity. In recent years the sight fills you with loss, evoking plastic trees and the peanut butter export trade. "You are local?" The taxi drivers always doubt, as they take you through the congestion on which you first learned to drive, so what do you say, are you ready to dust off the fine film of soot that has encased you?

Anywhere else, you live a separate life unprotected by irony. Your dreams are exposés that allow no distance between yourself and every single felt emotion. Cross all the cities' limits, get out of bed, and repeat history. You will want yourself all over again, once you diminish the size of your own warnings.

You head out toward the rainforest to find a clearing. Look in—an ocean rises.

IN EVENT OF A PLUNGE, GIVE OVER TO YOUR BODY

Two days after we came home
                    with a bitter pineapple

            I dreamed you   scooped out its black
eyes one by one   threw out the
    core

black eyes but where
did the black
eyes go

                                             & we sucked on
                     one sweeter end

                   I can't bear your sour
                green in my gums   rescue me this acrid shear

me shear me
   shear
   me shear
   heat of stricken   tongue
          ohgodyesing
   into double-eyed glaze

I keep waking keep turning
turn over to catch your spit's   arc

a heart can tube out to fit a cylinder if a heart
can lengthen why be happy when you can be
normal

this is all practice   anticipate
a fresh
-born face turned
up with want

you want me caught cheating

          want me
      grating bent asking   want

me contemptible you
    want me when I close

    my eyes   everything resumes its original
form   the pineapple watches

                from the windowsill, whole & unsliced
          & thrilled

                by this brown winter
                where nothing ever
                happens
as if frozen

in time
    you only love me when I
deargodhelp

GOOD NIGHT, FALL IN—

poem for David

Then it ends   with we
laughed as a panic response laughed through
crowds strangling chrysanthemums
white flowers   between the
years past   years
still searching eyes   searching

for the air you circulated as   dead seriousness

here   they drape a white sheet over you
here   the trees hunch and sequester
here   you sink soft to stop-lit-go
here   your nails blue into solid fact
here   I learned how

words bitten
off regrow
with the same precision you
counted out your days

I traded in all my childhood games to give you my single stroke of luck

To remember no more than a speck of color after it ends   It ends

with your smile falling the way the long day curves   a long line of
me and me and me   queued up beside

       someone dropping
  a head in sorrow   for wanting to unearth the dead
      You don't pivot because you
  make decisions as if laying down feathers
      ready to fly away at any given moment

                 a head dropped in hope while I make

grayscale photo
copies of your away-forever face

      I make another girl of myself
a girl hey   a girl is
calling out between
  you and you
behind you   I lay

you   I lay you to rest in your most beautiful shirt

ALLUSIONS AGAINST TIME

All my poems that end in you end in dreams of drinking
        the sea

Tomorrow I will wed you all wrong & plunging

    as if gravel   released from a stern cliff
                               Tomorrow
let's
sire lies kept away from us

& I will nurse at my heart every
        offspring

                of faith & pluck:

how many more ways can we dangle as bait?

        & everything I insist on
will distill down to

a bean-sized
universe nesting in the palm of my hand

When we walk I drop behind your footsteps

It's me
who picks up leftover existences
                every impossible gaze

      the vilest metaphor of a storm's eye,   barely a dent against the weather
            Tiniest pulse of a fish gut

Tomorrow we hide

in one of four   corners of the ocean
     Tomorrow forget the sea has floors   Tomorrow in your faded jeans
                              I'll start digging for your song's underbelly

     Tomorrow no sun to desiccate our sick stench

          Tomorrow winds slicking our wet faces

     Tomorrow pass me off as dead undeparted

Tomorrow if in death everything in me settles where it belongs then

     Tomorrow I need & need another day more

POSTLUDE

Some people come and some people keep staying
to map discarded locations of every
breast song inside me but I can't come on easy pleasure.
Stone of no specific grade or a time scale
ringing in my ear just like that. In our relationship
of ejecting each other's solstices, sickness
right out of my breath,
all I could think of was the closeness of holding a sigh,
not for fear of its breaking, only that sometimes
gentleness is utterly optional, how
above the safety of burnished touch
I just want an unwinding so thorough
its centrifugal force cannot
be located, this world where fish beneath a stream
spit out bubbles clearer
than all those mornings we have forgotten,
and with a wrench in my heart
I want to make a new
documentary
about the natural world, about love, about
blue weekends, and I want to investigate
alternative endings for us, want to
find out more
about the weather,
about where to catch a heavy rain,
about why clouds drop from the sky,
about the resemblance of wonder,
about what to wear on days like this,
About how to walk outside to
fall into the world—

THE USE OF LYRICISM

This morning, the dim skies are halting
the passage of time. An error in the weather.
I am in two places, torn between the clouds
outside and some photos on my screen.
James Baldwin's former house in the South of France.
The first thing the developers tore down was his writing
studio—to make way for luxury villas they will name
"Le Jardin des Arts," bidding up to thirty million dollars.
Only the Jardin will not be Baldwin's garden,
will not have the round table at which he took
reading breaks. Three years before his death he admitted
"I certainly have not told my story yet." This mimetic silence
drums with hope, waiting to sound out in the many
more decades he thought were to come.
"It's hard for me to recognize *me*," he said.
"The way the world treats you is unbearable."
Le Jardin des Arts will carry luminous myths
of Baldwin the artist, stripped of any locatable color
or weight. Popular psychology keeps pumping out optimism
via anecdotal studies, see how art can save lives even if it kills
its maker. Baldwin wrote of someone questioning Miles Davis
giving money to Billie Holliday—why did he do it
knowing she'd just spend it all on heroin?
"Baby," Davis only said, "have you ever been sick?"
and that answer stretched into the most buoyant footpath
I'd ever set my feet on, never mind where it led or came from.
I don't think it's as simple as temptation that pulls us out
every time the street ahead turns a dark corner. You could master
your destiny every waking hour and the bell curve
will still get you at night, that's how Thatcher was dead
wrong to say "there is no such thing as society &
people must look after themselves first."
The biological essentialist argument for selfishness
flew out the window the moment the first human
carved a piece of dead wood into the likeness

of the animal she was supposed to hunt, and who did it
neither to attract a mate nor to generate food.
The task of creating representations
of reality drove a quivering stake into the ground that day,
and have since doubled as an abandoned
pilgrimage site for theorists who make grand claims
about utility or victory or hardwired instincts, as in
every time I walk my dog toward the Mississippi
levee I have to pass a shiny plaque that reads
FREEDOM ISN'T FREE. Who knew violence
struggled to believe in its own surety and sought
for comfort too? The theater of imperialism is always
weeping over its self-inflicted wound, while I stroll
away my days trying to become everyone's best American girl.
Even the most compelling means of escape winds up
being just a metaphor—after the house is dismantled and
the invasive weeds rooted out, were you supposed to
transcend language and never worry about falling in love
with your aggressor? Sometimes on these long walks
I try to trot with light steps for fear of putting
too much bodily pressure on this earth,
because what would I do with anything more?
Holliday had seventy cents to her name
at her deathbed, her liver rock hard and bleeding
out at forty-four, a fact unconcerned but completely
entwined with what the world had done to her.
Without greatness she'd written, "Don't explain... /
right or wrong don't matter," and I imagine her voice
rising up round and fat and pomegranate-sweet,
billowing toward the clouds
up where I cannot see.
Today's heaviness is already thinning out,
ready to fall again as rain

I want to help you like this world.
I can help you like this world.

NOTES

1. "When translation fails, displaced identities easily become worthless beings" is adapted from a line in Don Mee Choi's *Freely Frayed...Race=Nation* pamphlet (p20).

2. "As for me, I am a watercolor. / I wash off." are the closing two lines from Anne Sexton's "For My Lover, Returning To His Wife" (p23).

3. The poem that begins "To ask for likeness..." is inspired by Alexandra Kleeman's short story, "Fairy Tale" (p30).

4. "If This is Not Possible, Live Twice" takes after Mary Ruefle's "Some Nondescript Autumn Weekend" (p51).

5. Frida Kahlo once said, "I never painted dreams. I painted my own reality," challenging the categorization of "surrealism" for her work in favor of a personal, autobiographical lens (p59).

6. The line "why be happy when you can be normal" is the title of Jeannette Winterson's memoir (p65).

7. "The Use of Lyricism" draws from Magdalena J. Zaborowska's *Me and My House: James Baldwin's Last Decade in France* and Aisha Sabatini Sloan's *The Fluency of Light* (p79).

Thank you,

cream city review, Juked, H_NGM_N, The Nervous Breakdown, TYPO, Yalobusha Review, Bone Bouquet, alice blue review, Twelfth House, The Rusty Toque, Matrix, West Branch, The Wanderer, Tuesday Journal, Winter Tangerine Review,

for first publishing many of the poems in this book, often in different forms.

Thank you, too, to Anomalous Press and Ahsahta Press, for first publishing some parts of this book in chapbook forms.

Thank you, human chuo, for permissions to this book's cover image.

Thank you to the supportive communities of *The Watering Hole* and *Squaw Valley Writers' Workshop*, as well as my beloved friends, family, confidantes, companions, passersby, heart keepers, teachers, and mentors.

And thank you, cherished editors at Noemi Press, for giving this book the love it was afraid to ask for, and pushing it into luminous shape.

Grace Shuyi Liew grew up in Malaysia, a postcolonial peninsula firing with desire. From there she learned rural escapism, sea breeze, migration, longing. She is the author of the chapbooks *Book of Interludes* (Anomalous Press, 2016) and *Prop* (Ahsahta Press, 2016). She is a Watering Hole fellow, and her other honors include the Lucille Clifton Poetry Fellowship from Squaw Valley Community of Writers, Aspen Summer Words scholarship, resident writer at Can Serrat in Barcelona, resident at Agora Affect, and others. She holds a BA in Philosophy and MFA in Creative Writing. She is at work on a novel, and Careen is her first full-length collection of poetry.

poetry // $15

Sharp in their vulnerability, the poems in Grace Shuyi Liew's *Careen* are injurious wounds, moving through a cavernous politics, breaking off, turning in, and restructuring memory as scaffolding, pain as terrifying recurrence. This work is jolting in its refusal to reign in its rageful grief. Shuyi Liew disarms language in order to disarm us, leaving us little room burrow in our fear.

Raquel Salas Rivera, 2018-2019 Poet Laureate of Philadelphia

Careen is a battlefield of conflicting desires, a place where words are dragged from the liminal engine of Grace's 'kinetically charged' soul into the broad daylight of racial politics. A place where it's impossible to dodge the inevitable bullets aimed at whiteness and its whitened landscape. Her work swells with infinite breast songs shaped to evoke and choke all exit doors towards a place where poetry doesn't exist as an aftermath. Her poetry is designed to stay current, to enrapture, and also a place to "reveal [her] private galaxy of bruises." Are her words bruises? Grace's *Careen* will drape a white sheet over you.

Vi Khi Nao, author of *Sheep Machine, Um[...] Hospital*, and *The Old Philosophe[...]*

To whom do you give the potential to seize the whole space of you?" Grace Shuyi Liew, of course. She brings it all: fairy tales and video games, fetish, sex, and politics, perennial mothers and daughters jumping off cliffs, global cities and statelessnesss. Here dreams are real, and worlds careen refracted in and across time. Go for the ride.

Gabrielle Civil, author of *Swallow The Fish* and *Experiments in Joy*

ISBN 978-1-934819-78-4

9 781934 819784

99990